NATURAL DISASTERS, WHAT & WHY?:
1ST GRADE GEOGRAPHY SERIES

Speedy Publishing LLC
40 E. Main St. #1156
Newark, DE 19711
www.speedypublishing.com

A natural disaster is a major adverse event resulting from natural processes of the Earth.

A tropical cyclone
is a circular storm
that forms over
warm oceans.
When it hits land, it
brings heavy rains
and strong winds.

Hurricanes form when warm moist air over the water rises, it is replaced by cooler air. The cooler air will then warm and start to rise. This cycle causes huge storm clouds to form.

An earthquake
is the shaking of
the surface of
the Earth, which
can be violent
enough to destroy
major buildings
and kill thousands
of people.

Earthquakes happen when two large pieces of the Earth's crust suddenly slip. This causes shock waves to shake the surface of the Earth in the form of an earthquake.

A tornado consist of a very fast rotating column of air that usually forms a funnel shape.

Tornadoes tend
to form from very
tall thunderstorm
clouds called
cumulonimbus
clouds.

A volcanic eruption is the point in which a volcano is active and releases lava and poisonous gasses in to the air.

Volcanoes
erupt because
of density and
pressure.

Tsunamis are large
and powerful
ocean waves
that grow in size
as they reach
the shore.

A tsunami is caused by the displacement of a large volume of water. Most tsunamis are caused by earthquakes.

An avalanche
is a rapid flow
of snow down a
sloping surface.

Avalanches occur when large amounts of snow fall from steep slopes due to a fissure in the snow pack or due to an accumulation of too much snow for the slope's angle.

Drought is
a period of
below-average
precipitation
in a given
region resulting
in prolonged
shortages in its
water supply.

Drought may occur almost anywhere in the world.